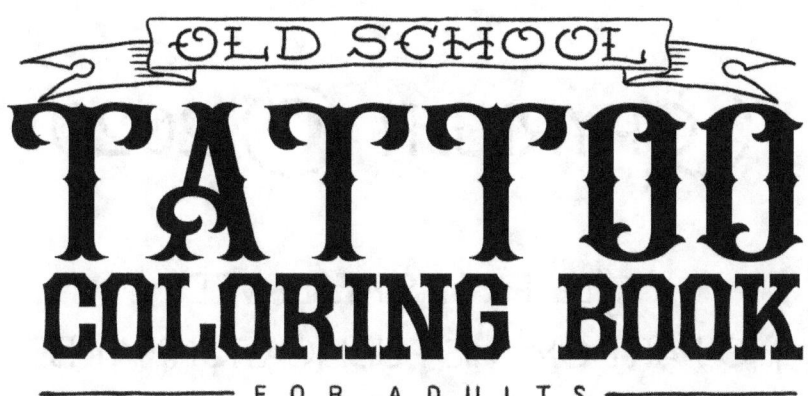

THIS BOOK BELONGS TO:

_____

COPYRIGHT © 2020

All rights reserved. No part of this publication may be reproduced, distributed, or transmitted in any form or by any means, including photocoying, recording, or other electronic or mechanical methods, without the prior written permission of the publisher, except in the case of brief quotations embodied in critical reviews and certain other noncommercial uses permitted by copyright law.

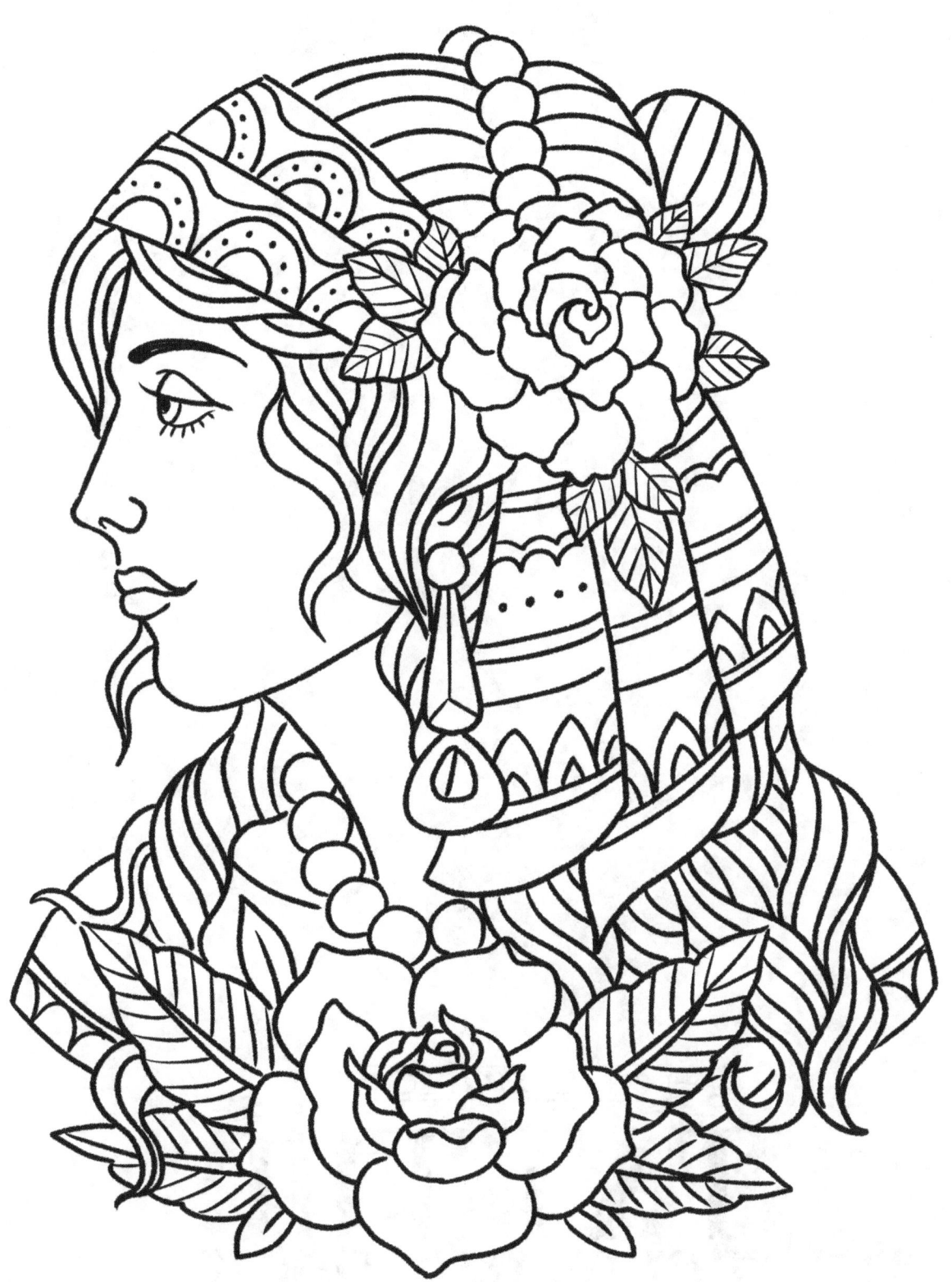

OLD SCHOOL TATTOO COLORING BOOK

FOR ADULTS

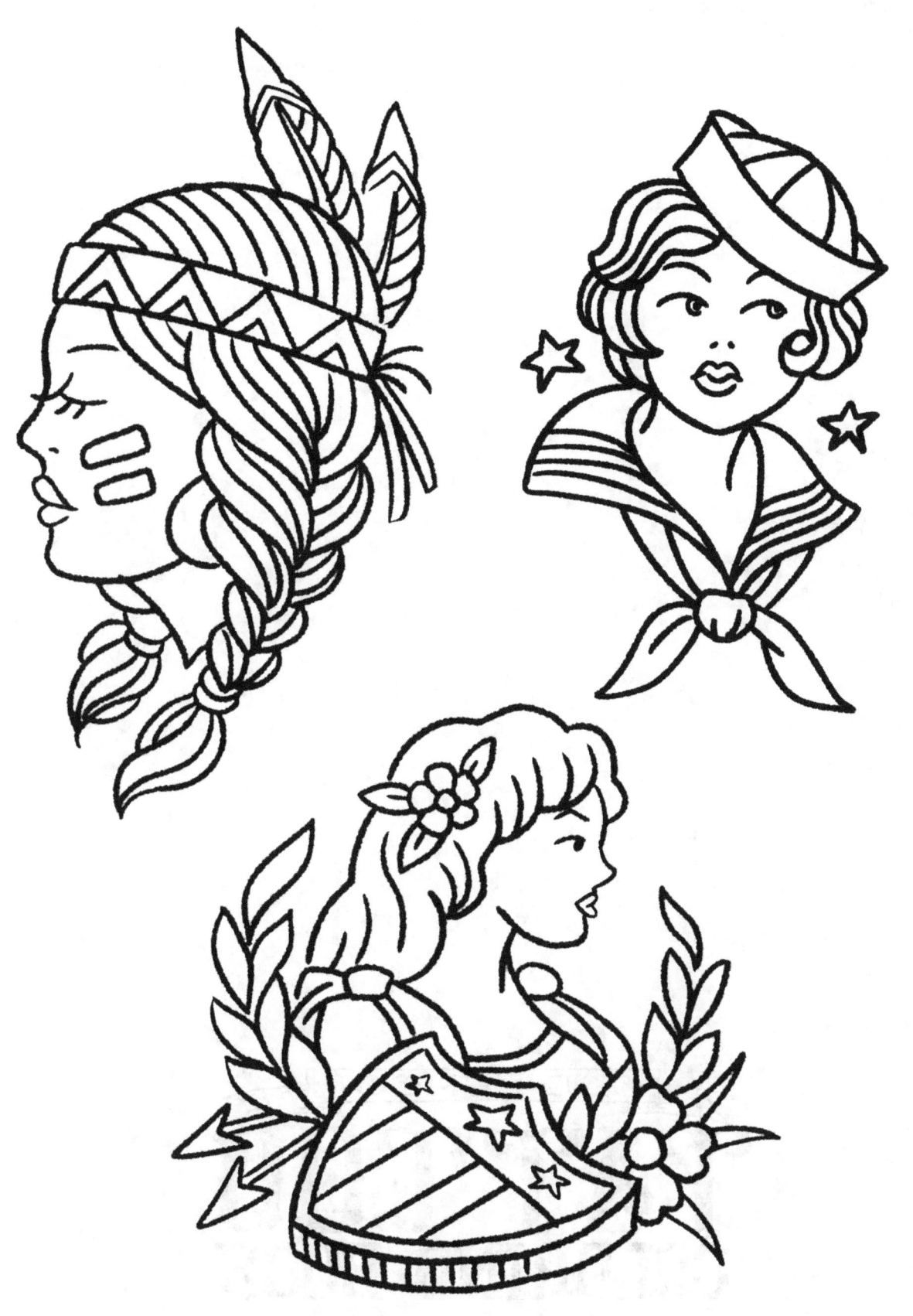

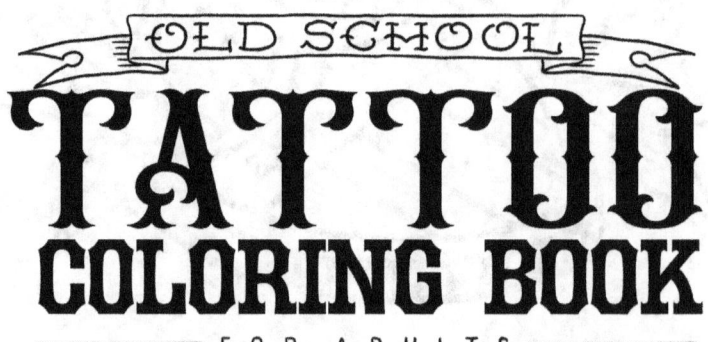

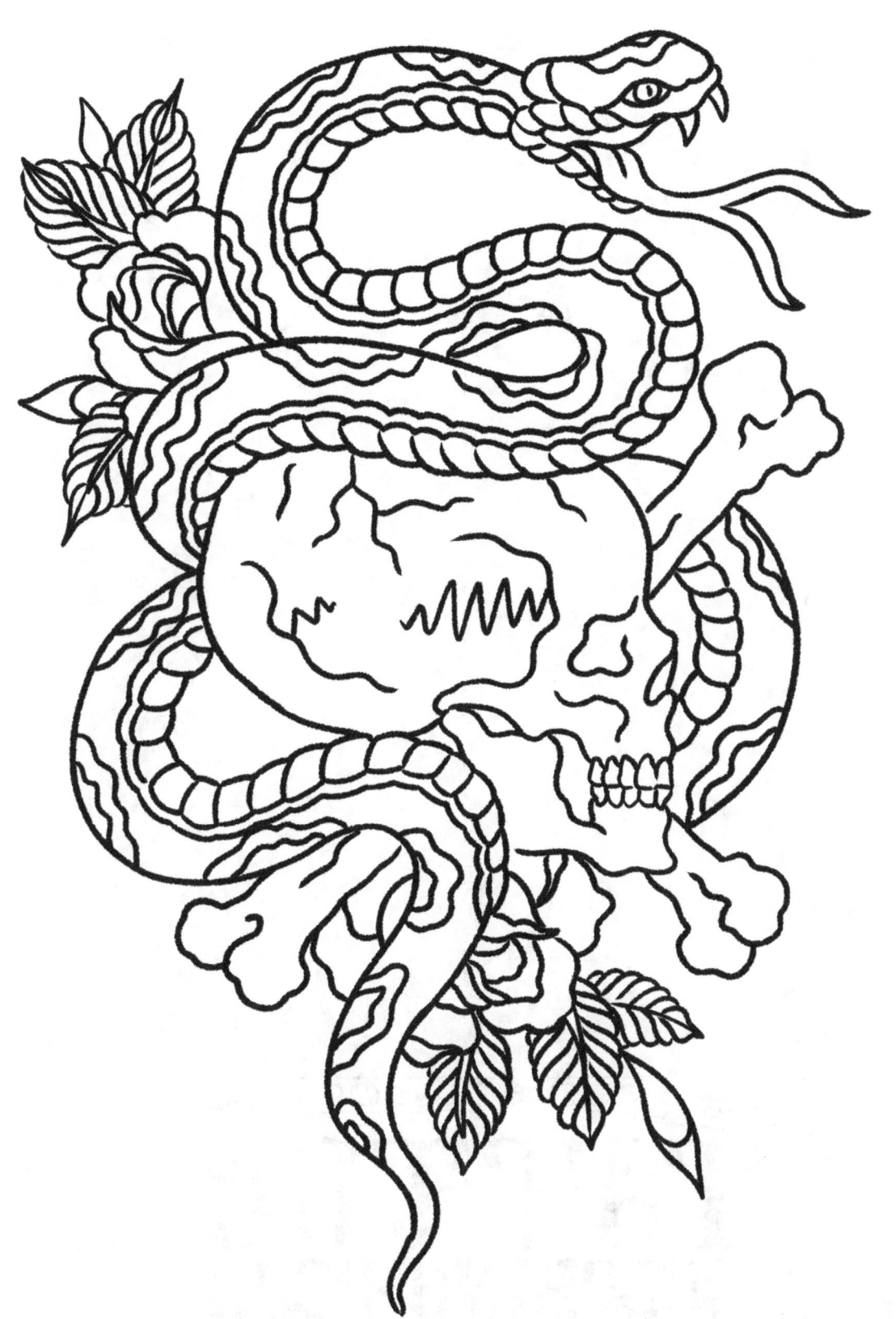

OLD SCHOOL TATTOO COLORING BOOK

FOR ADULTS

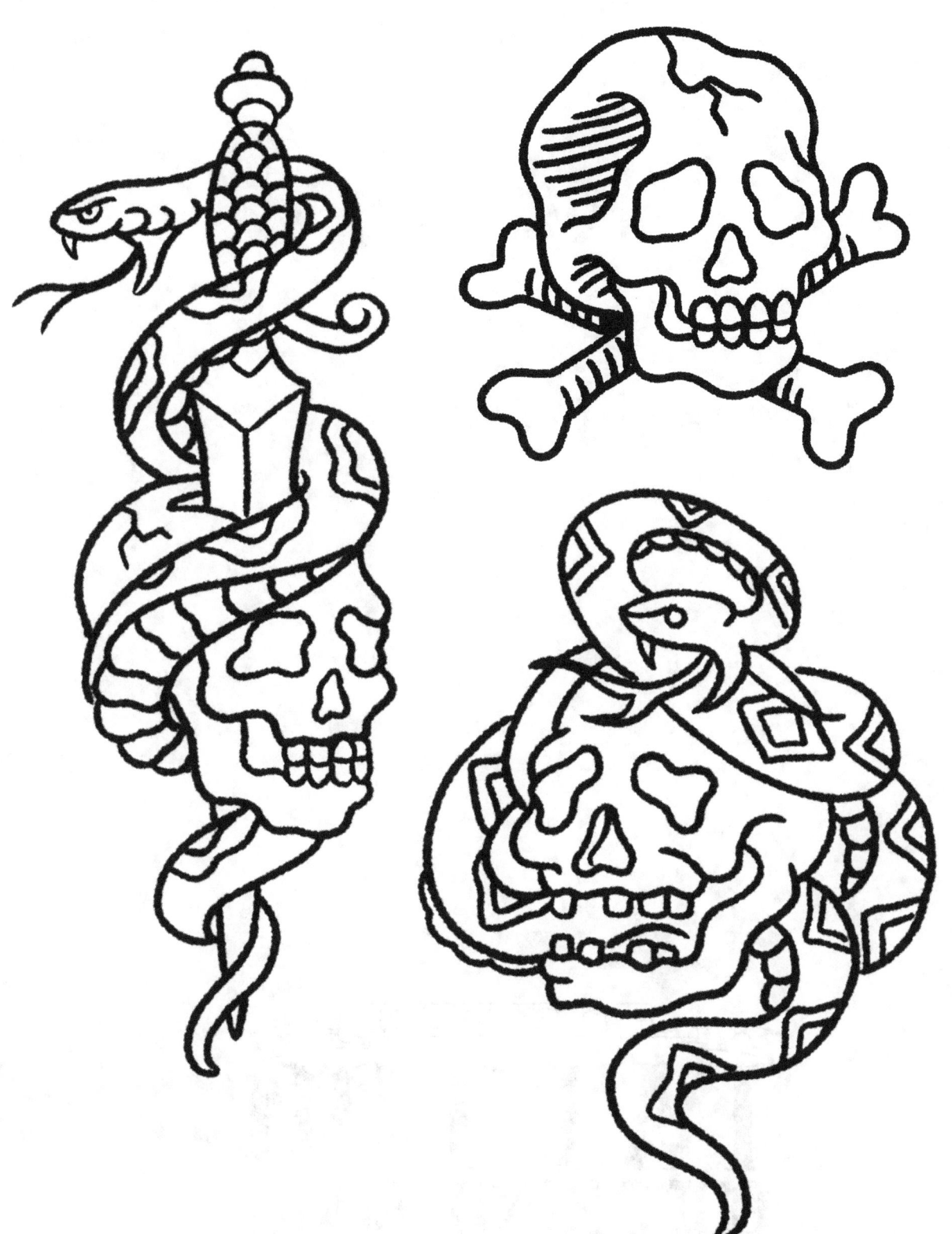

OLD SCHOOL TATTOO COLORING BOOK
FOR ADULTS

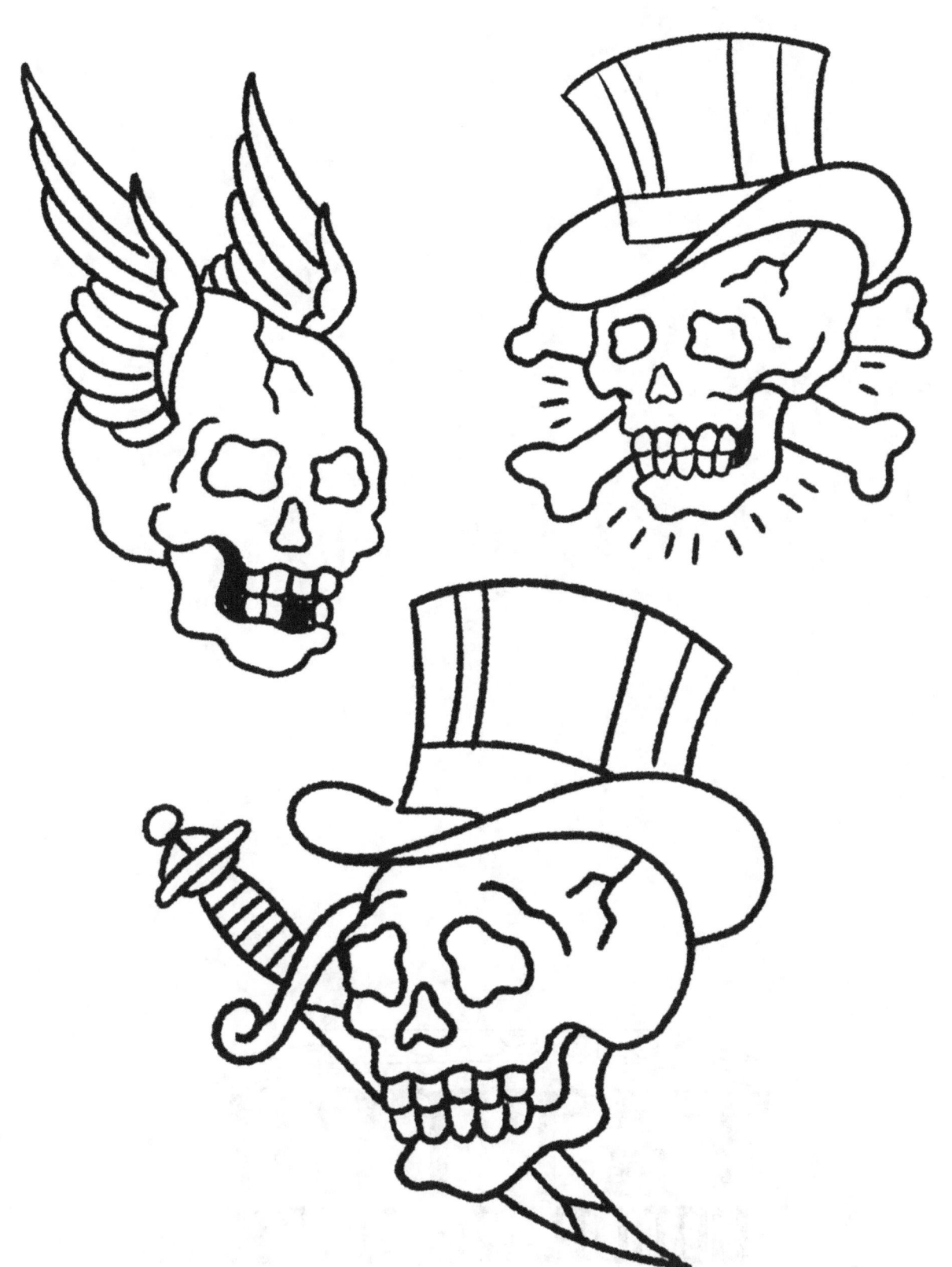

OLD SCHOOL TATTOO COLORING BOOK
FOR ADULTS

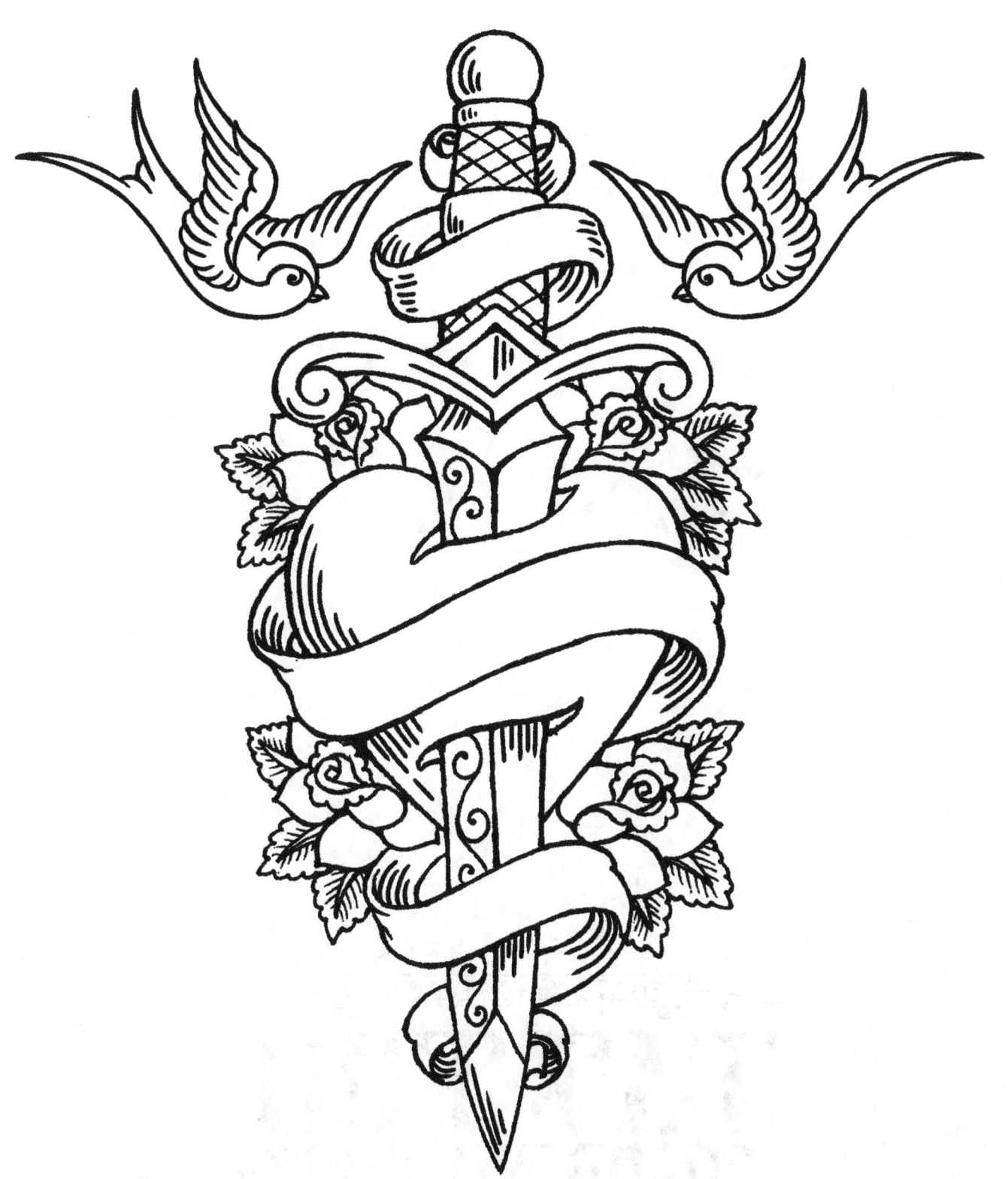

OLD SCHOOL TATTOO COLORING BOOK
FOR ADULTS

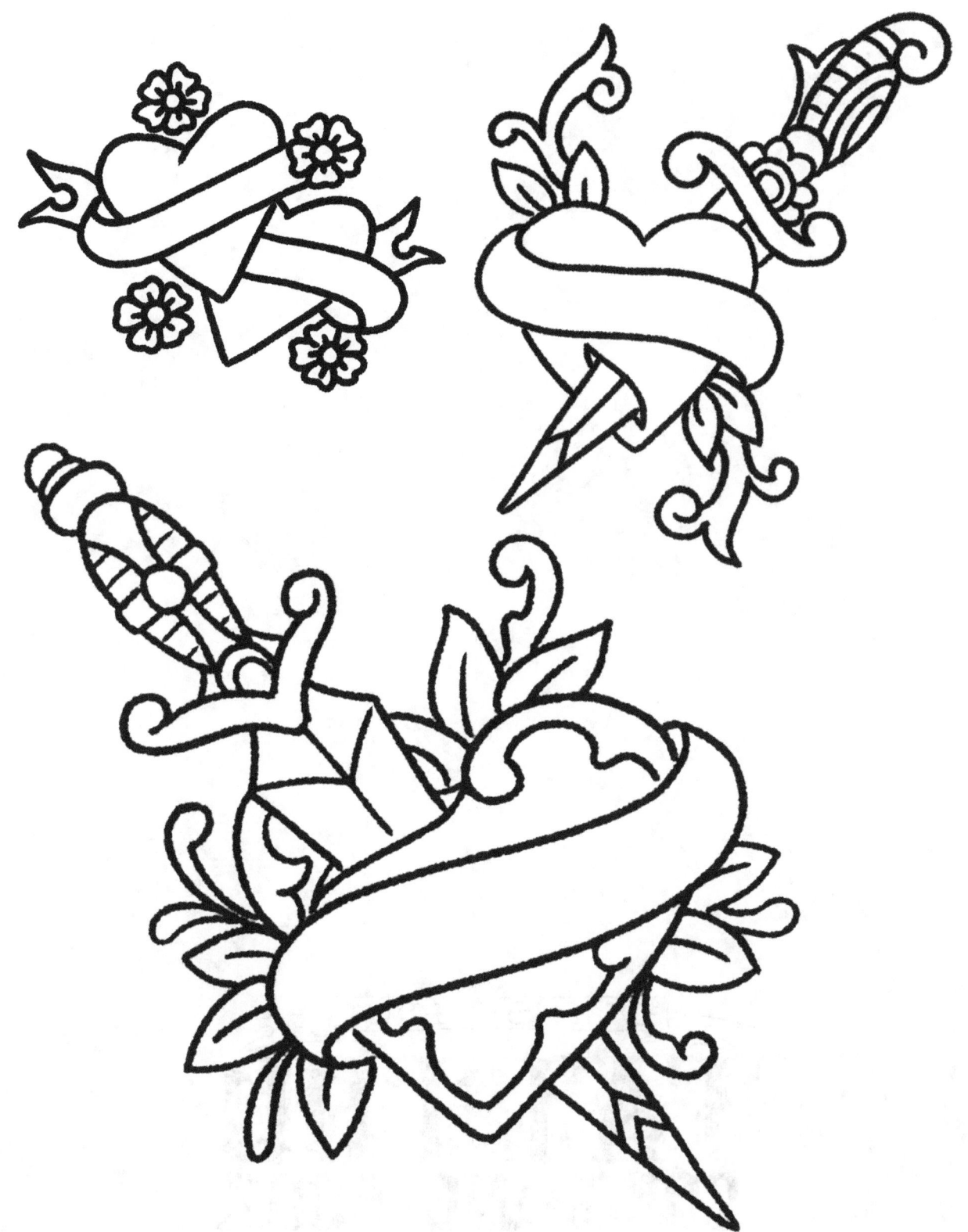

OLD SCHOOL TATTOO COLORING BOOK
FOR ADULTS

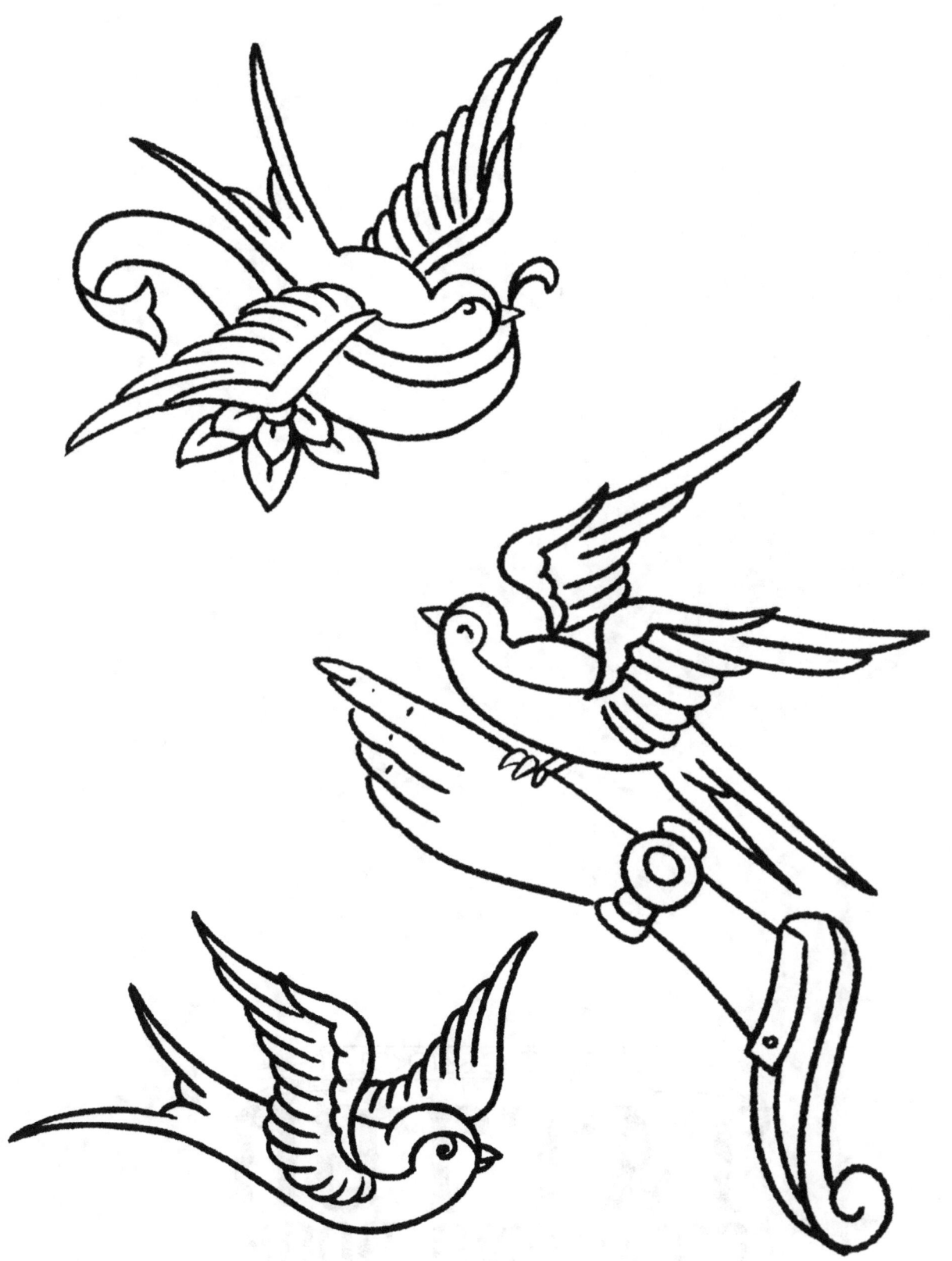

OLD SCHOOL TATTOO COLORING BOOK

FOR ADULTS

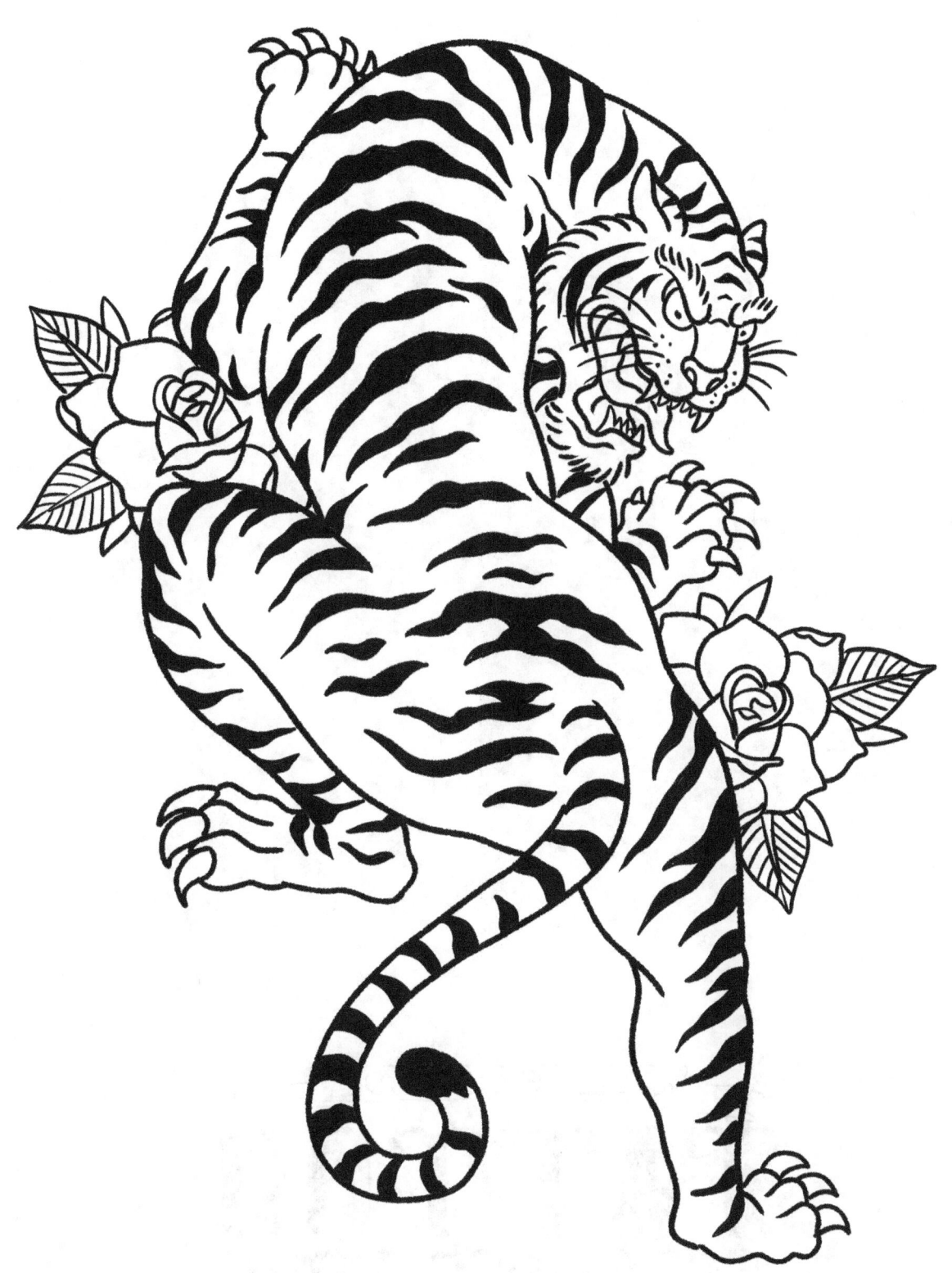

OLD SCHOOL TATTOO COLORING BOOK
FOR ADULTS

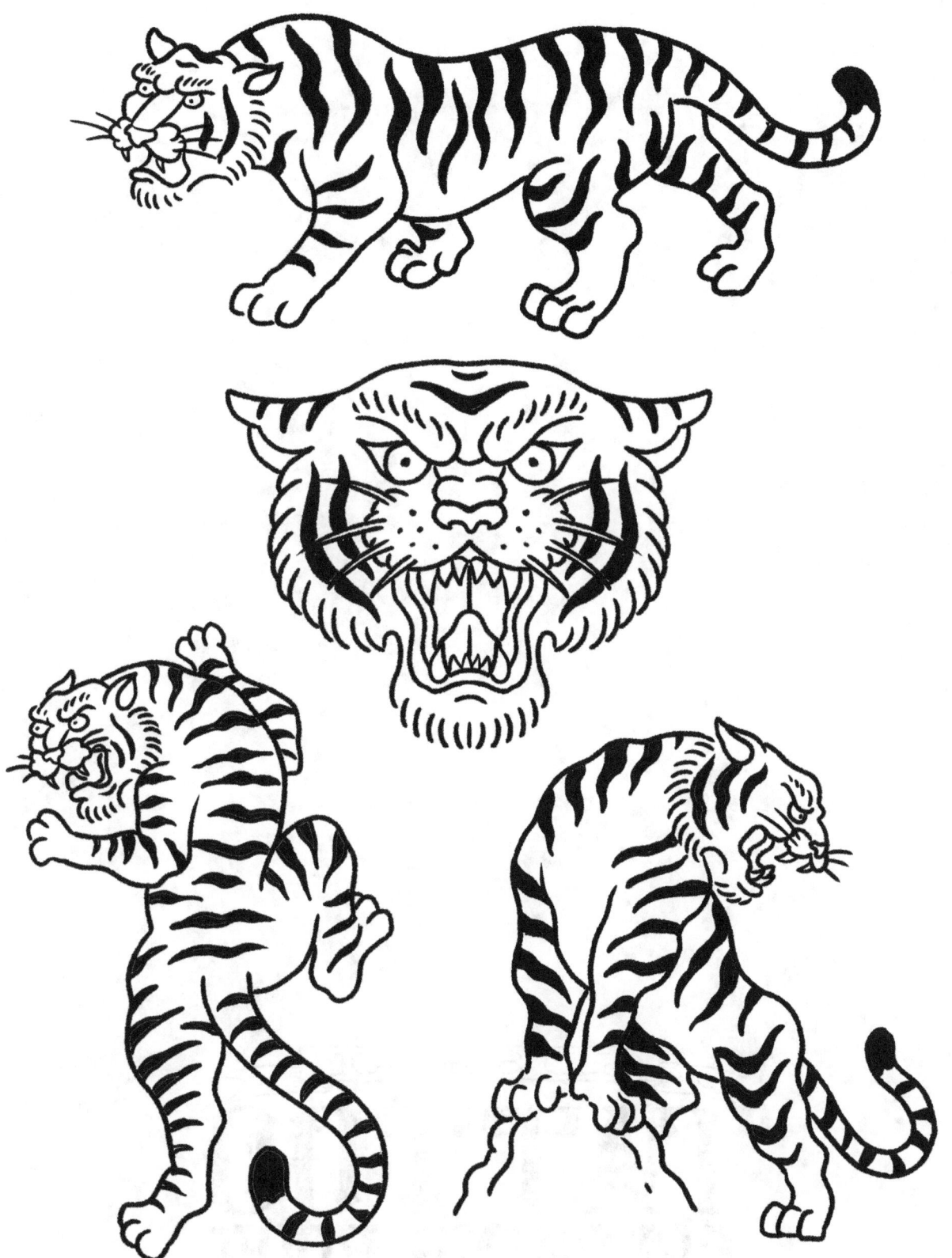

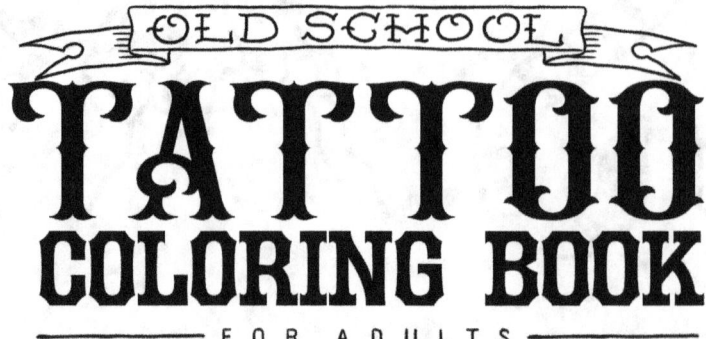

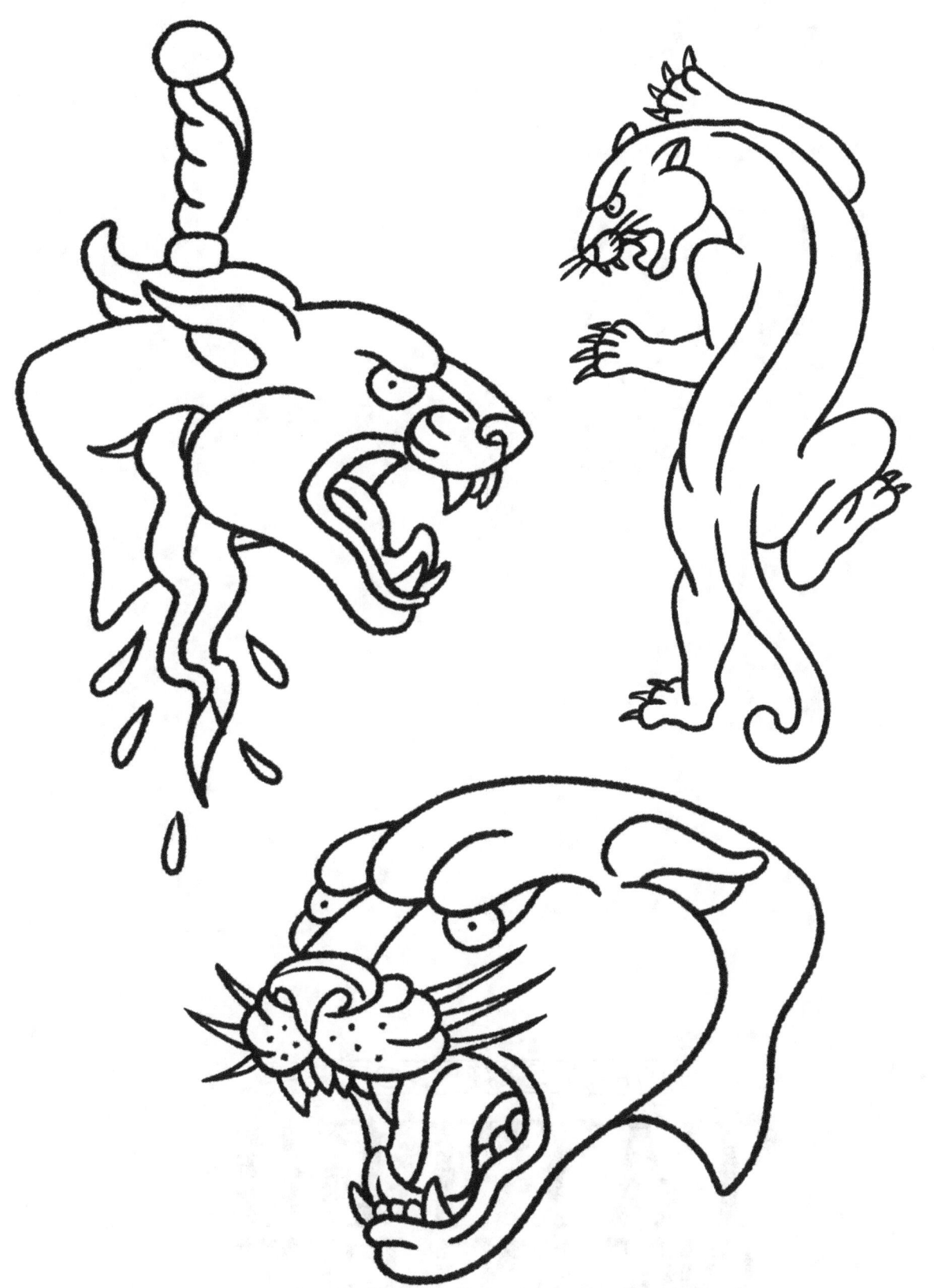

OLD SCHOOL TATTOO COLORING BOOK
FOR ADULTS

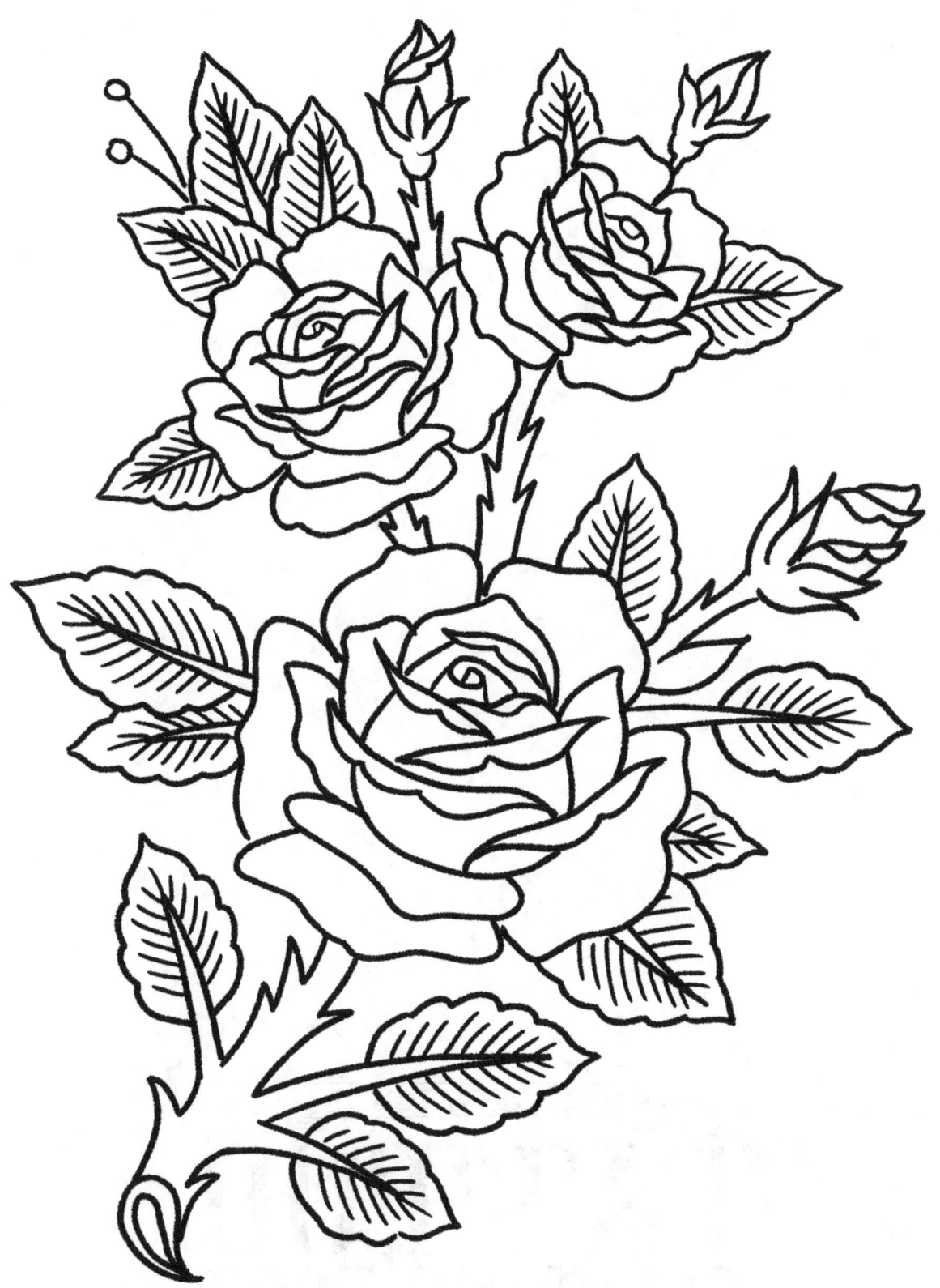

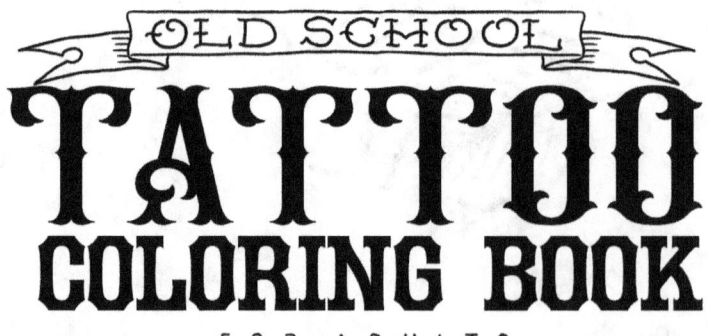

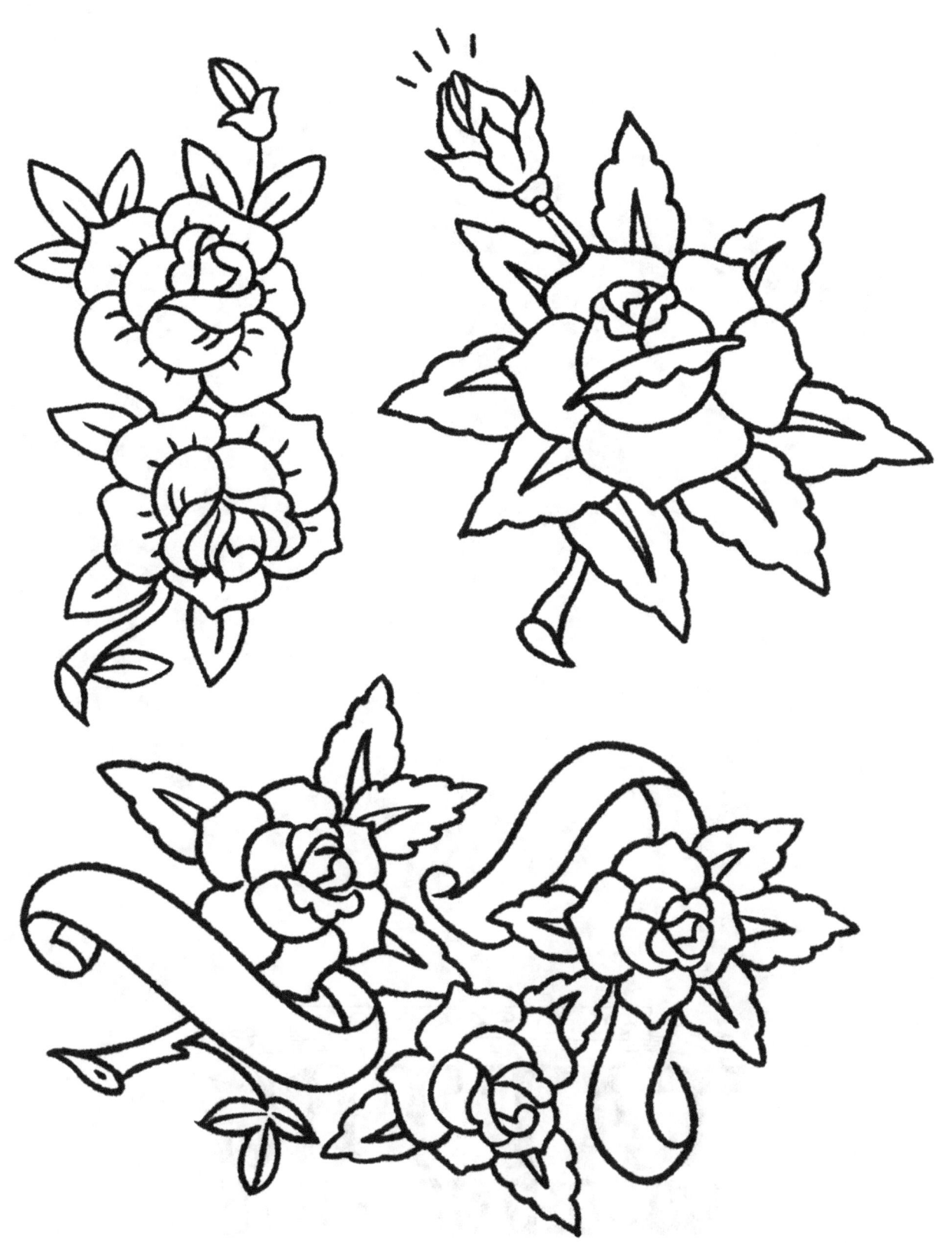

OLD SCHOOL TATTOO COLORING BOOK
FOR ADULTS

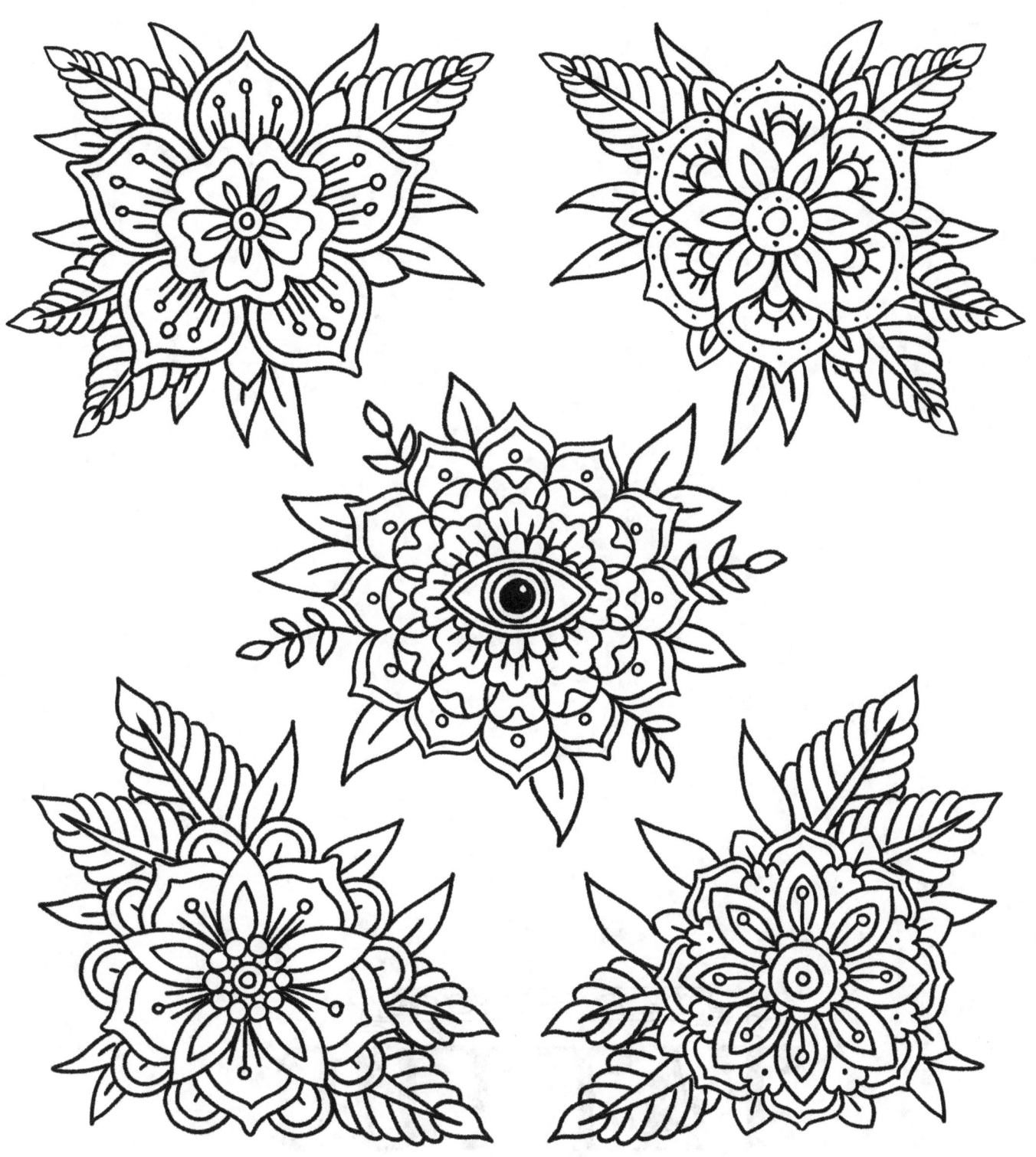

OLD SCHOOL TATTOO COLORING BOOK

FOR ADULTS

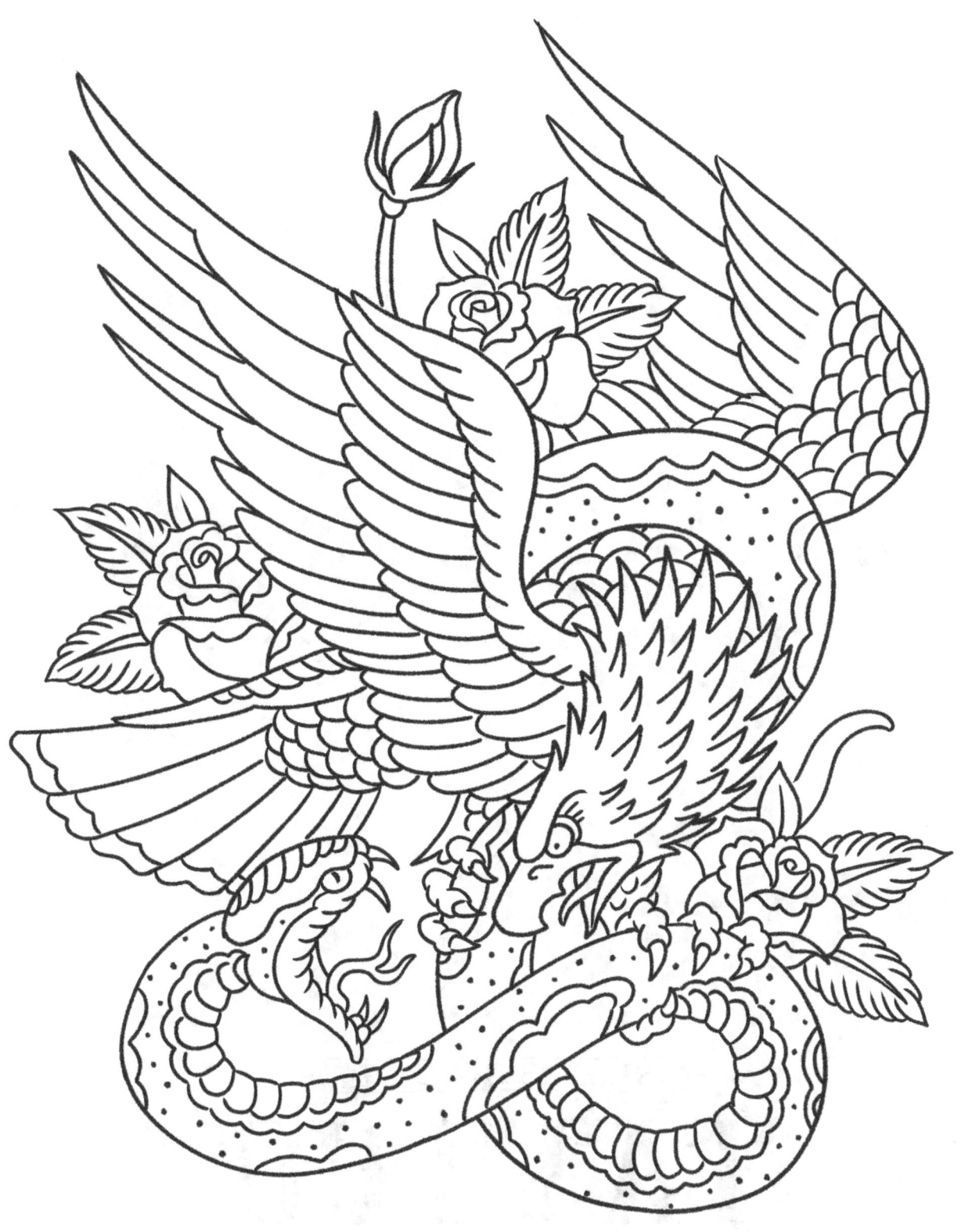

OLD SCHOOL TATTOO COLORING BOOK
FOR ADULTS

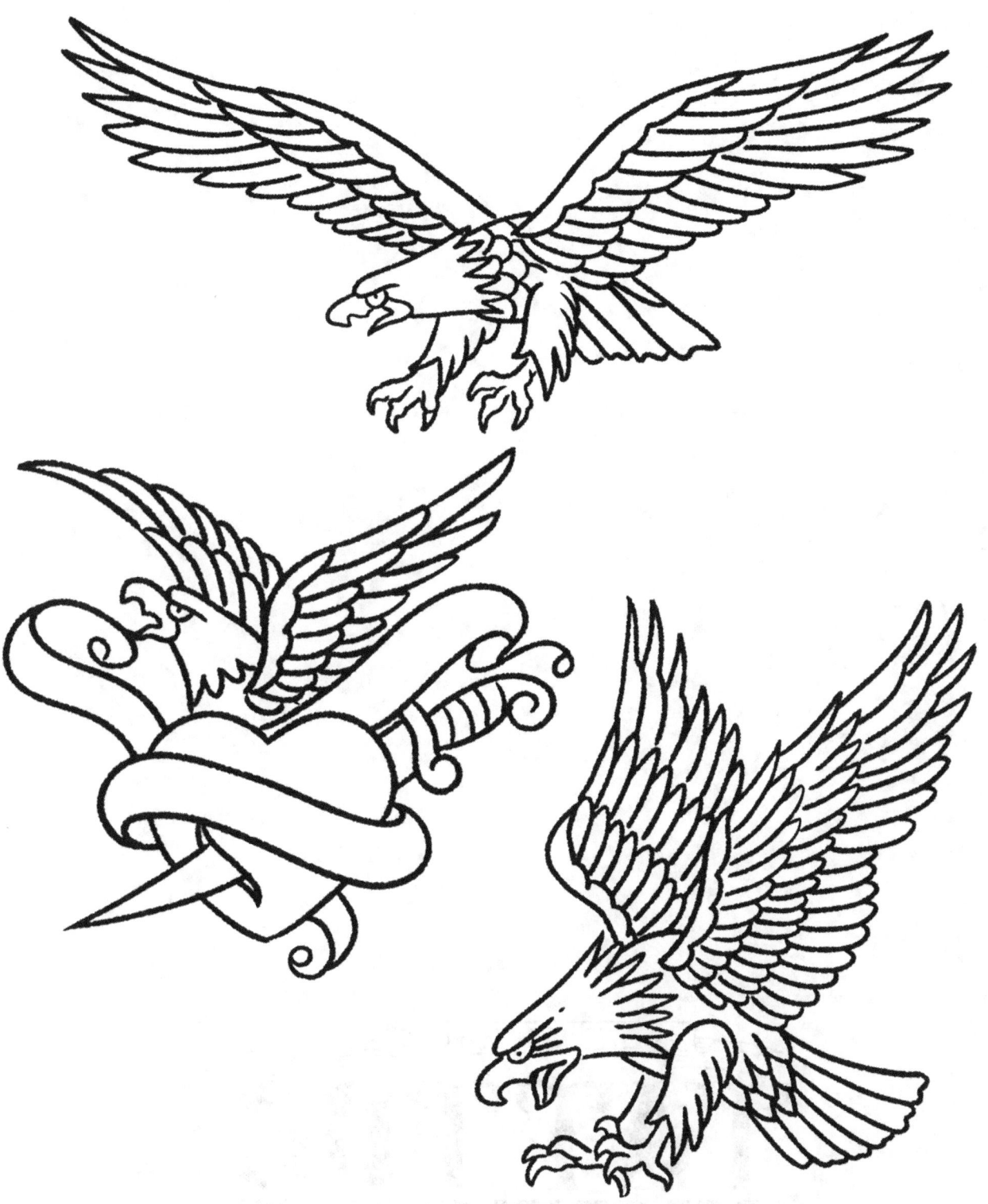

OLD SCHOOL TATTOO COLORING BOOK
FOR ADULTS

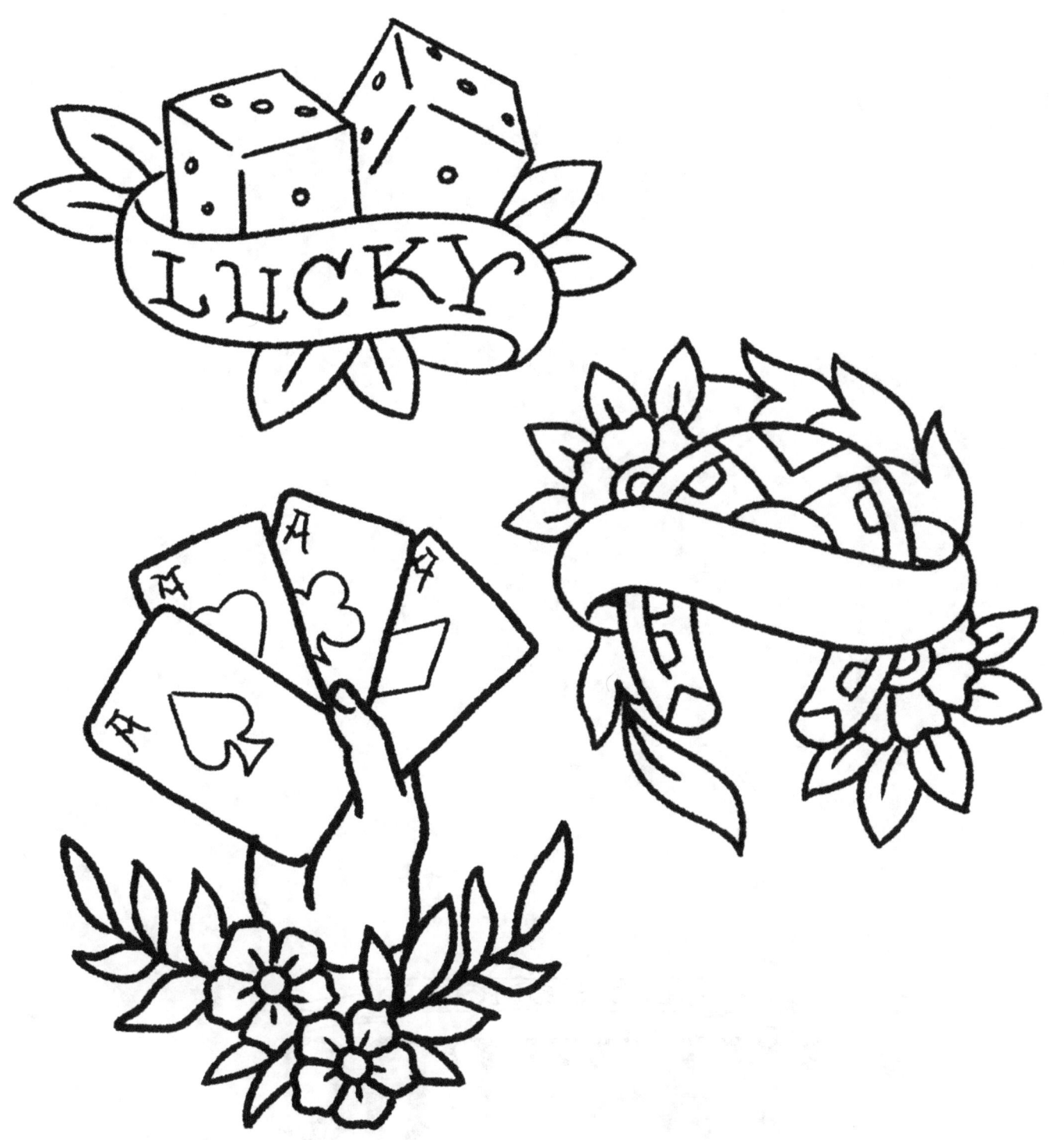

OLD SCHOOL TATTOO COLORING BOOK
FOR ADULTS

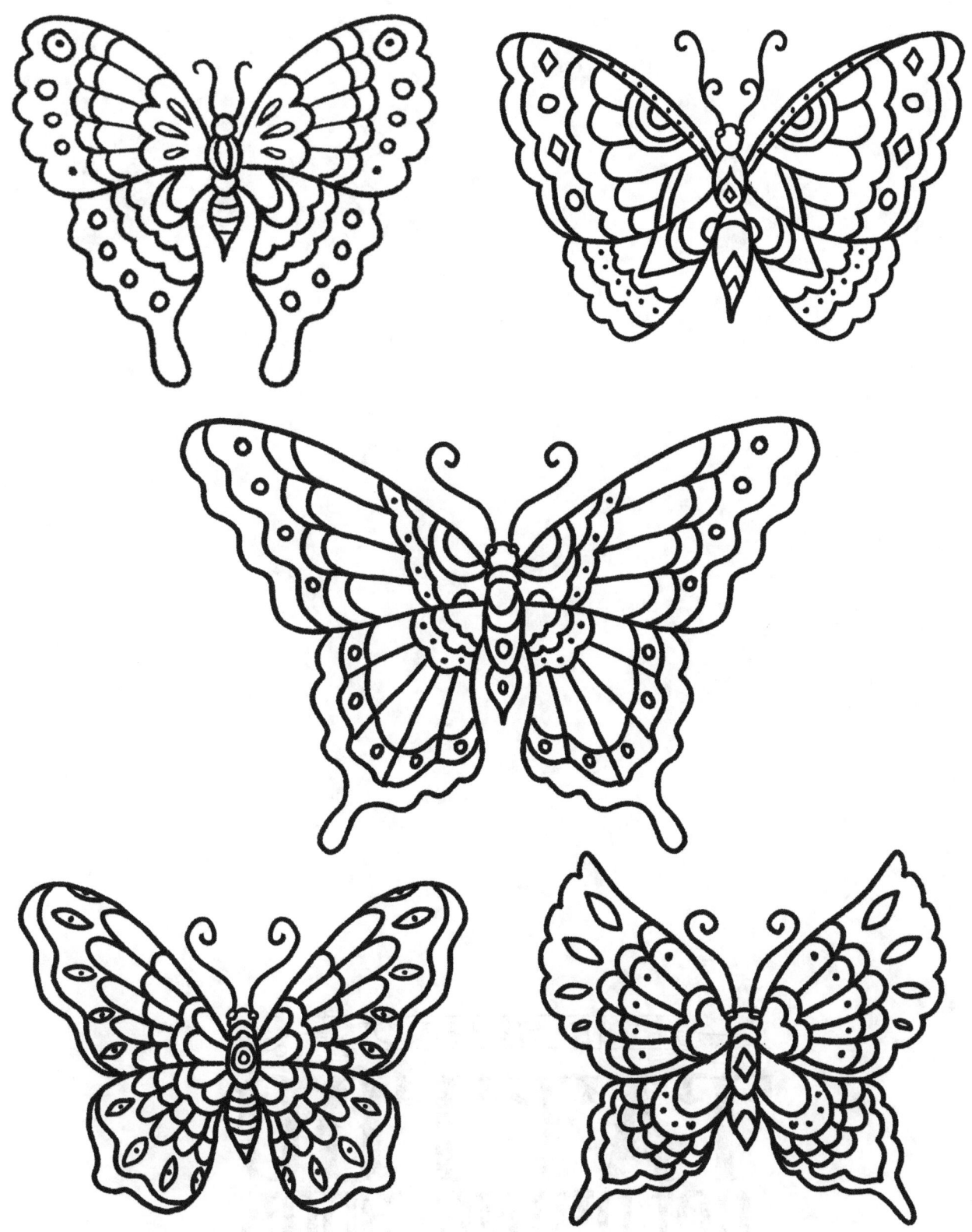

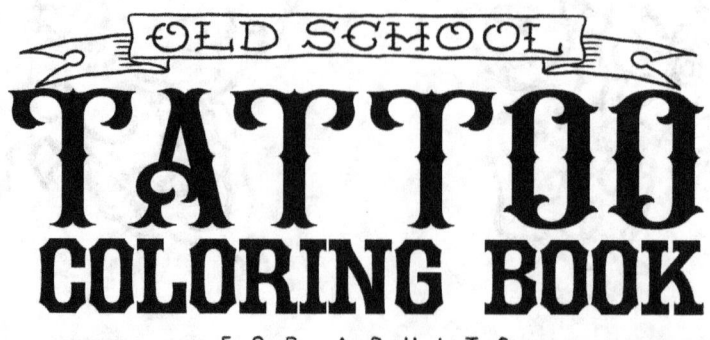

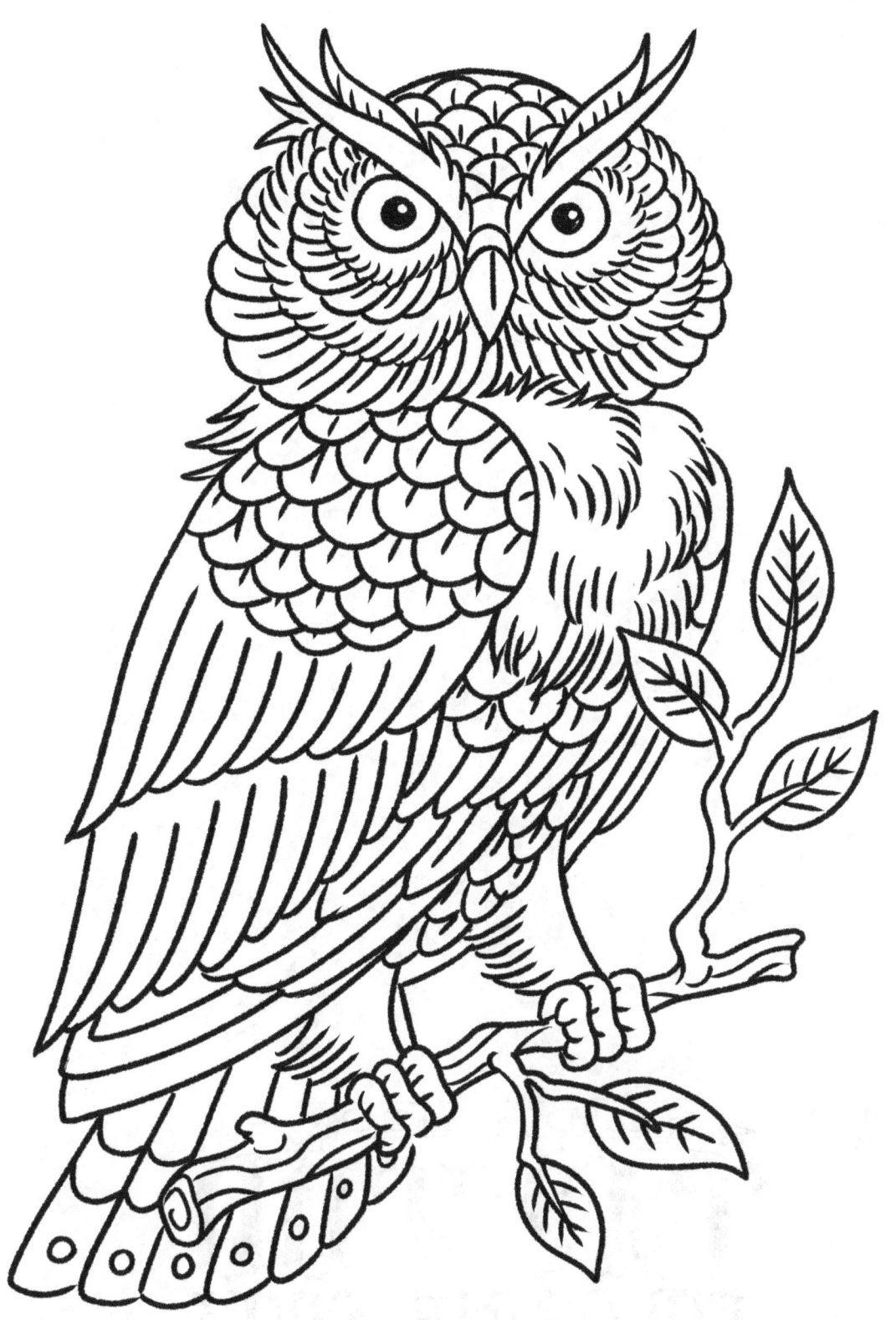

OLD SCHOOL TATTOO COLORING BOOK
FOR ADULTS

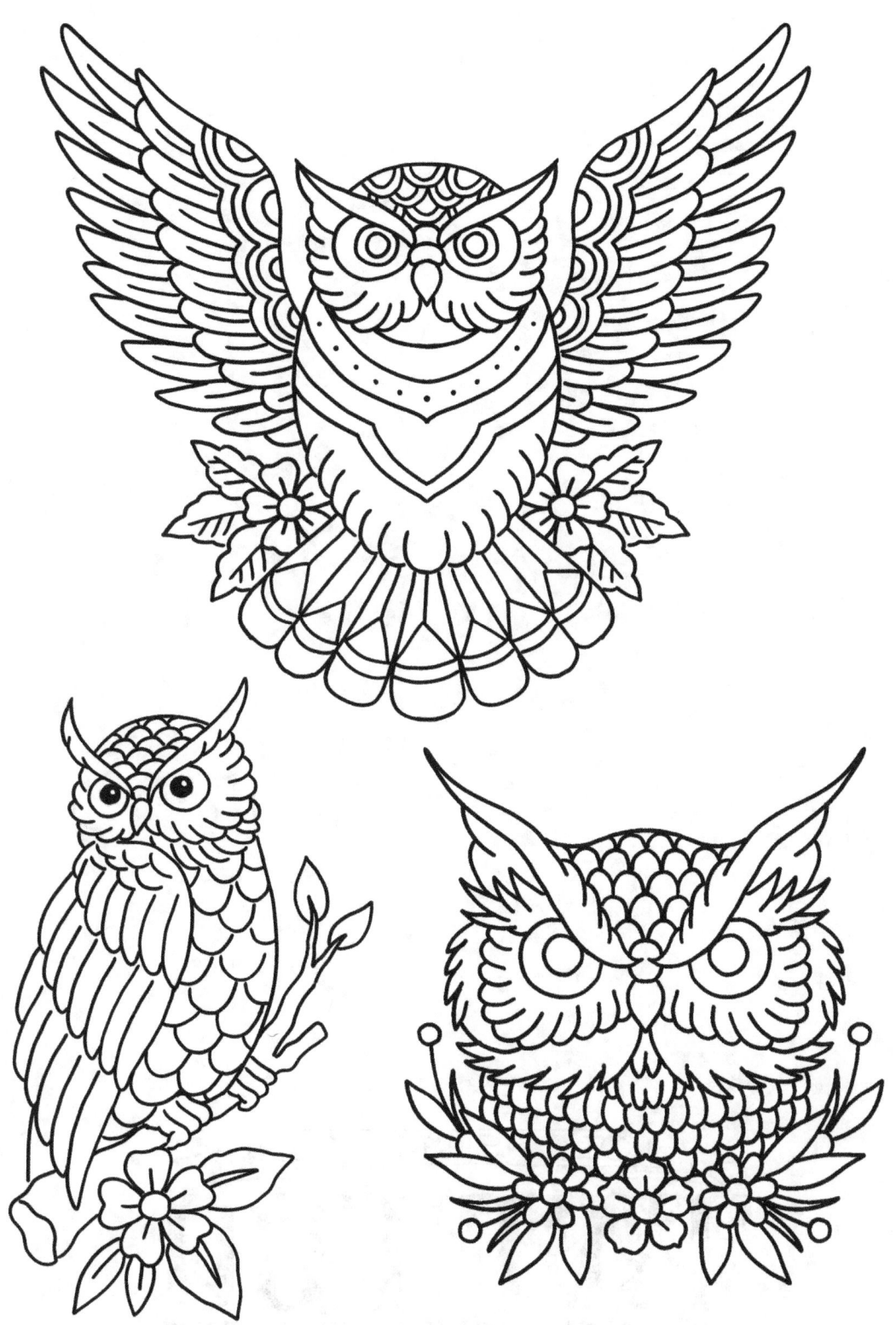

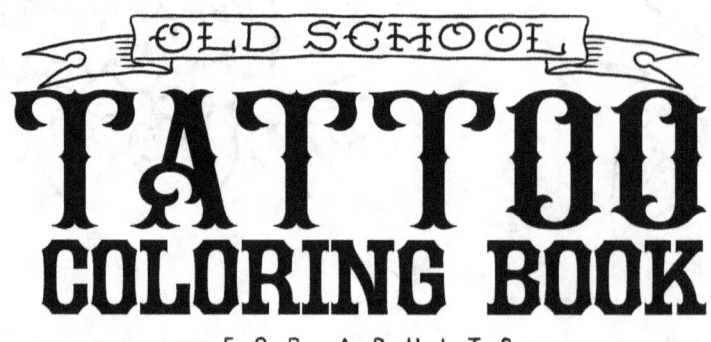

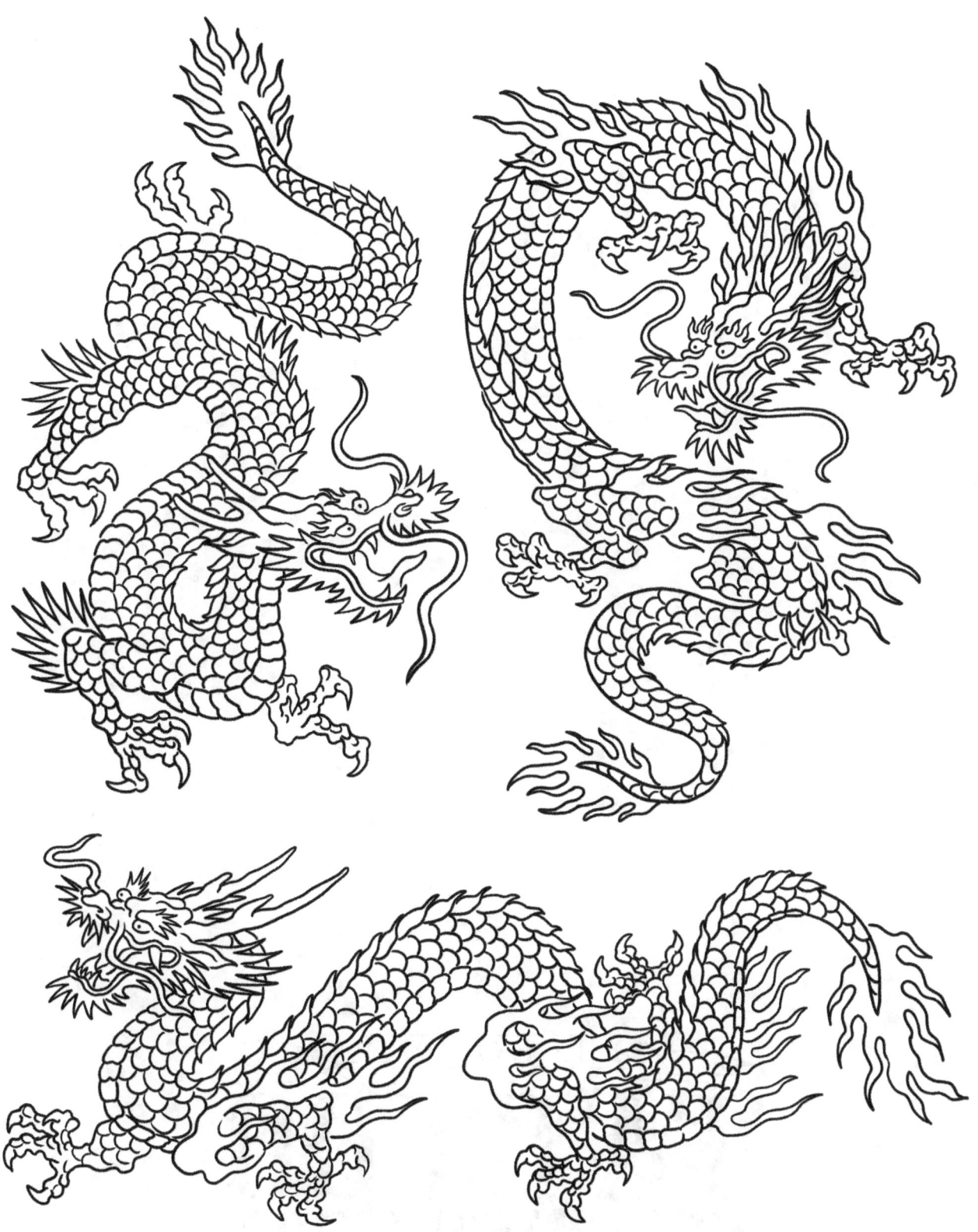

OLD SCHOOL TATTOO COLORING BOOK
FOR ADULTS

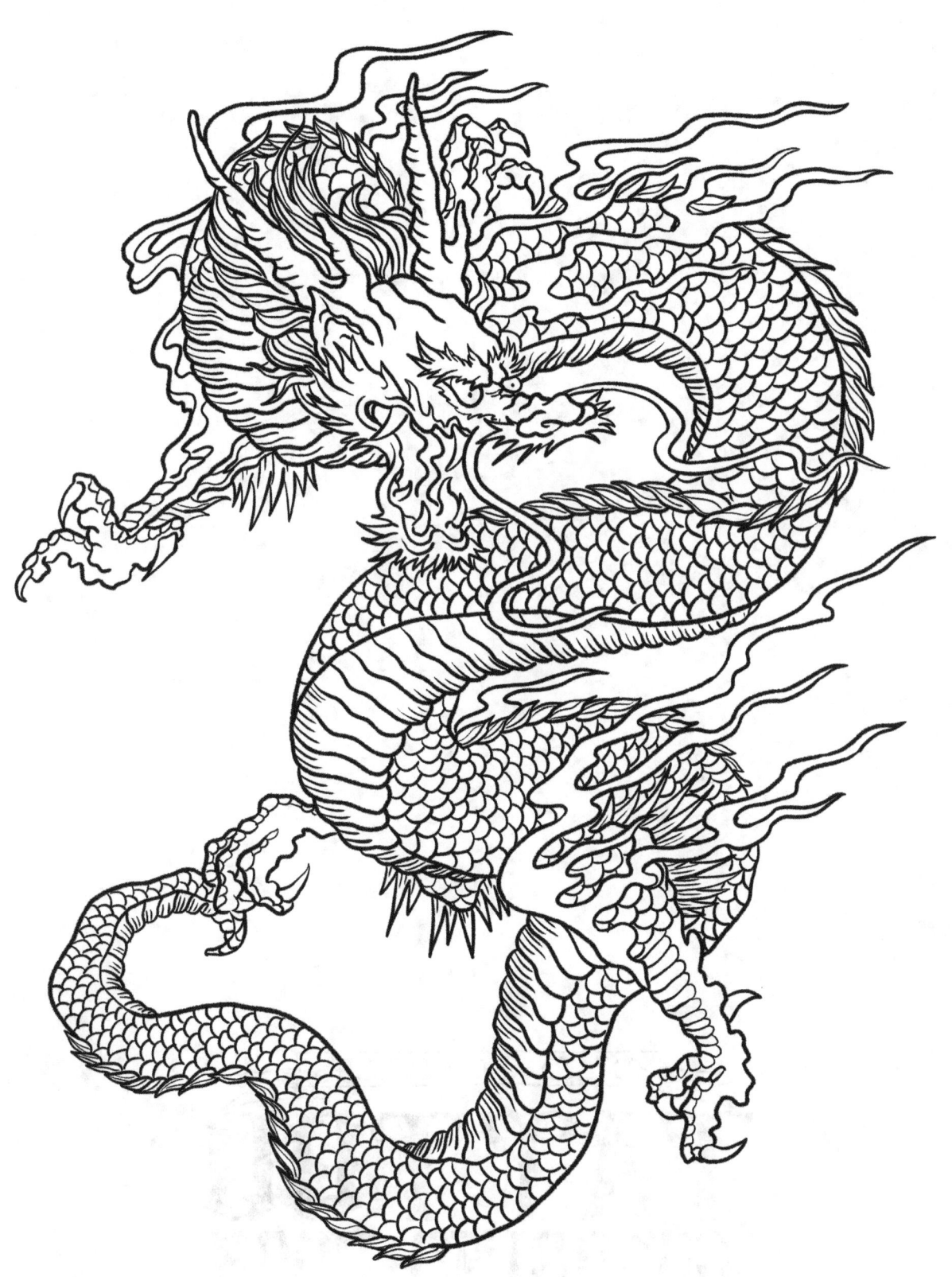

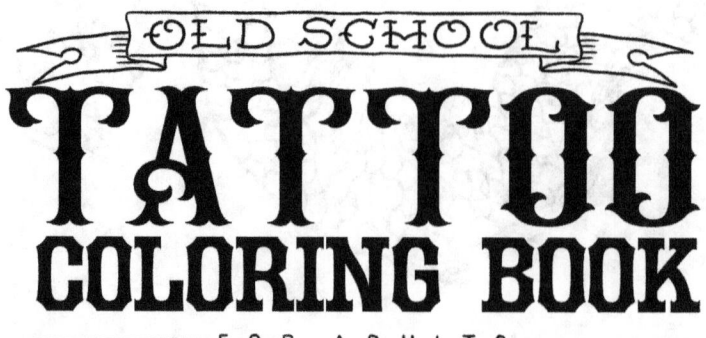

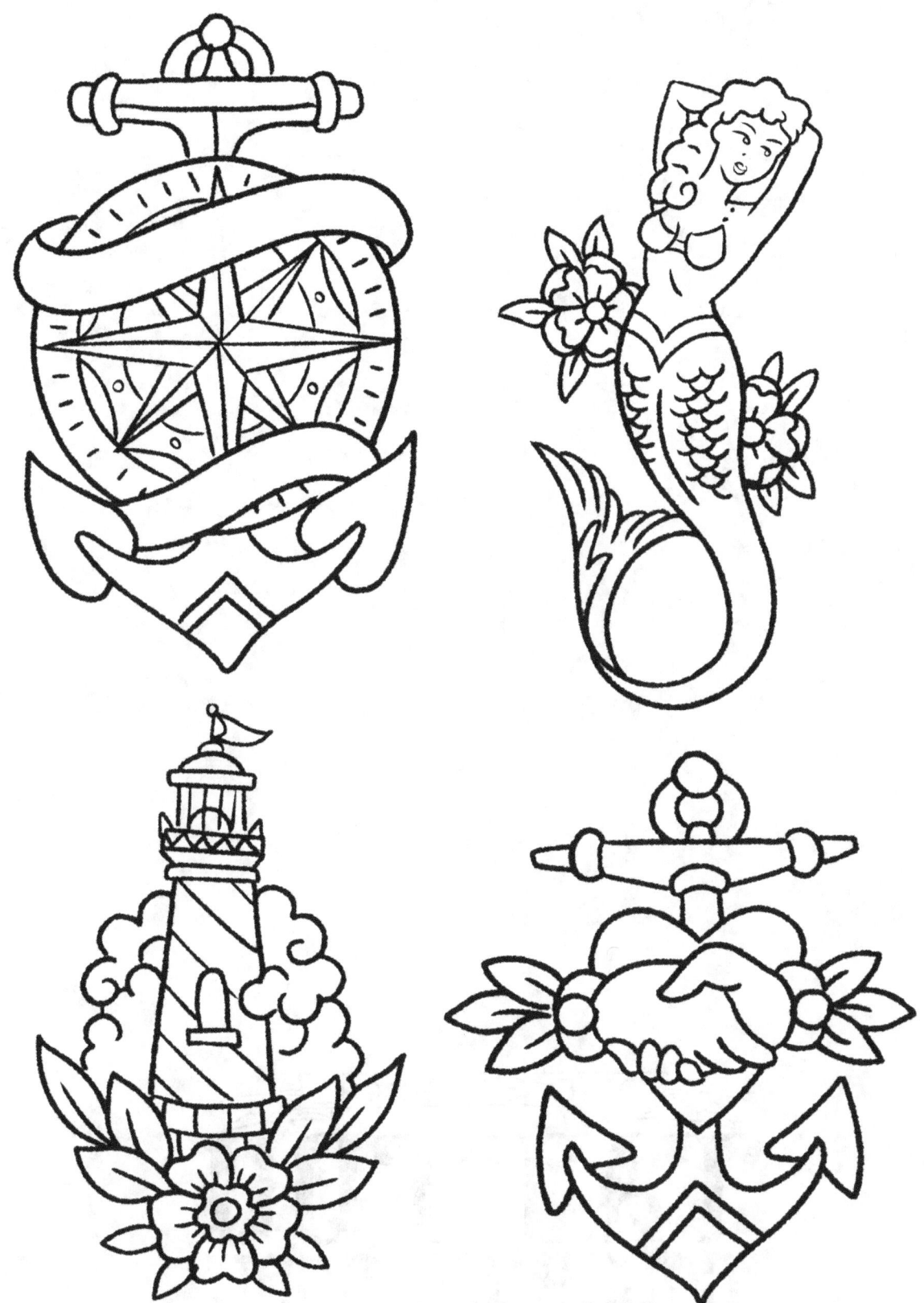

OLD SCHOOL TATTOO COLORING BOOK
FOR ADULTS

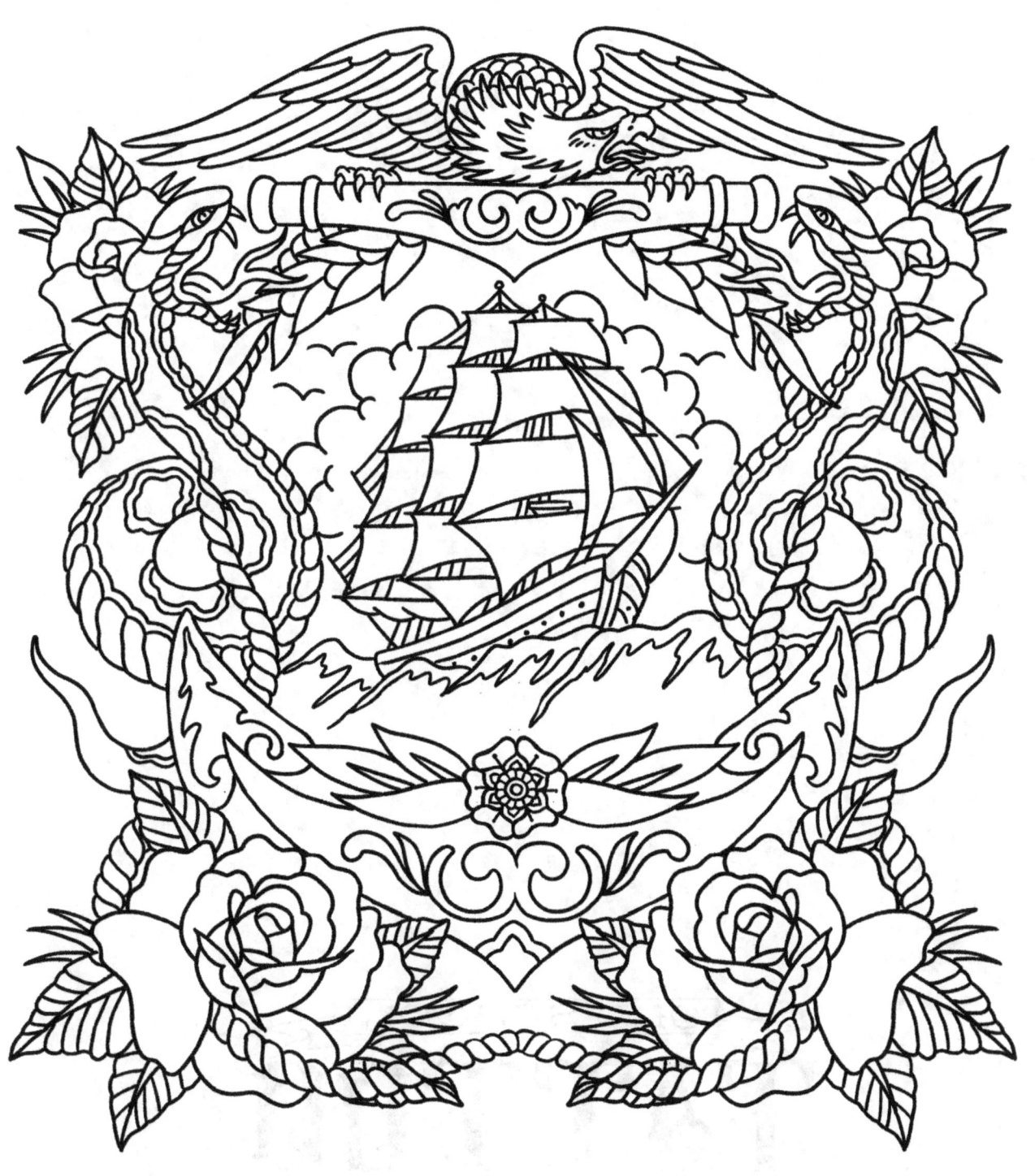

OLD SCHOOL TATTOO COLORING BOOK
FOR ADULTS